Don't Go ; Stay

Other Books by Deanna Repose Oaks

Life Span: A collection of poetry (105 poems)
Poetic Reactions (42 poems)
Trauma's Death (30 poems)
Inner Thoughts: Poems Suitable for Middle School (60 poems)

To purchase these books, please visit Deanna's website at:

https://deannareposeoaks.com/

Or ask about them in your library or local bookstore!

Don't Go ; Stay

By Deanna Repose Oaks

Cover Design by Deanna Repose Oaks
Book design by Deanna Repose Oaks
ISBN-13: 978-1-956482-09-6 (paperback)
Published by View from Room 217, LLC
www.viewfromroom217.com

Dedication

To Ruben, thank you for staying with me.

Table of Contents

Author's Note

There is nothing fancy in this book. 99% of the text does not contain stylized fonts. There is no artwork. Every line is left-aligned so that the line breaks and spacing are clear.

The only fancy thing in this book are the words sewn together poetically, and one poem about art.

Please take your time reading these poems.

You do not have to read every poem and you certainly do not have to read them in order. Enjoy what you can, when you can, save the rest for later.

If you or someone you know is struggling or in crisis, help is available. Call or text **988** or chat 988lifeline.org. Caring counselors listen and provide free and confidential support 24/7.

988 | SUICIDE & CRISIS LIFELINE

Donate to 988 prevention efforts here: https://988lifeline.org/donate/

Don't Go

You matter more than you know
And I need you to stay, not go
I don't want you on a slab, cold
I need your smile, to see you old
I need the warmth in your eyes
Hidden behind painful cries
I need the sound of your heart
Which beats its own pure art
I need these things in the world
I want your sadness unfurled

But these are things I want and need
And in this, I know I'm full of greed
But I can't help all my selfishness
If it starts you toward beyond nothingness

My words are here to hold you tight
To get you through this horrid night
I hope they light your way
To get you through, come what may

If you find me out in this world, please say hello
I will be so glad you stayed; I don't want you to go

1

Longed For Words

These are words I wish I heard
    You are loved
    You are amazing
    You are wonderful
    You are beautiful

Instead, I heard words filled with disdain
Words I cannot write, evoking feelings I can't explain
Full of hate, jealousy, anger, resentment
Words that rhyme with hazy or itch, or sucker, or....

I can't go there, not even in my mind
For it grants them power, makes me rewind

I heard these other unnamed words so often, from so many
That I now reject the words I wish I heard so plenty
    You are loved
    You are amazing
    You are wonderful
    You are beautiful

Or, worse yet, I replace
    You are loved
    You are amazing
    You are wonderful
    You are beautiful
With these unnamed words I can't say, write, or think about

So while you say these words I long to hear

I DON'T

I hide away in fear.

Today I found a path around these words
Now I say them to myself, so I cannot reject them or discount
   them or disbelieve

I AM LOVED
I AM AMAZING
I AM WONDERFUL
I AM BEAUTIFUL

Never-Ending Grace

I give grace
To the middle-schooler who bites my head off before breakfast
To my kids who forget to thank me
To the new wait staff at the restaurant learning the ropes
To the driver that tailgates me
To the person with the shopping cart that didn't see me there
To the cashier who rang me up wrong, twice
To my exes who changed the very fiber of my being
To everyone who has ever hurt me: emotionally, physically, or
    accidentally
To children who are just learning to be
To the elderly who can't remember who they are
To the person who cut the line in front of me
To my spouse who forgot to pick up that one thing for dinner
To my friends who don't call
To my friends that do call, but only to complain
To my family for being my family
To everyone who deals with my bad moods

I give people grace, as much as I can
Because I have little knowledge of their life's struggles
Their struggles could be deeper, wider, more painful than mine
Their struggles ALWAYS different than mine
For I can only see life through my lens and my struggles
Which I would never put upon someone else

I give grace
And every time I do
I give myself mercy

Which allows me to give more grace because
I need to do onto myself as I do onto others

Authentic Self

Am I the person they say I am, the person I most fear?
Or, am I the person I think I am, no matter what I hear?
The scales can tip, depending upon my day
Sometimes, I am just who they say
But only when my back is against a wall and I am caught
Otherwise, I am not

OR, am I just telling myself it's okay
To NOT be who they think I am today?
I question this because the words they use
Such words I always refuse
Seem to span distance and time
Appear without reason or rhyme

But they are the same words
Even though the first one died
Before the last one lied
These words inflict the same hurts

Do they speak some cosmic truth
While I point and say "You have no proof!"
How can I truly believe the who I am you see
When I can't find my authentic self when I look at myself to find
    me?

I Am Not

I am not suicidal, although my poetry tells you so
I am not suicidal because I learned long ago
That my pain and anger and sadness may stop today
But not for others, others I don't notice throughout my day
For there is a light inside, buried within my turmoil
That someone sees each day, whose loss will spoil

I know that flicker of light is there, so I can't put it out
You have that flicker too, of that I have no doubt
Sometimes it is buried so deep, behind a black-out curtain
Believe in that light, have faith when you're not certain
Because there is someone who is looking to you
To help them see their day through

Wrapped up in your blacked-out darkness, where you can't see
That your flicker of light is a beacon of hope, even to me

More Than Space

You do more than take up space
You fill this world with your grace
Even if your grace is just a heartbeat or two
It reverberates into the world around you
Filling in beats others might have missed
In your grace, you do assist
Because those beats echo beyond what you know
The effects may not help you see or grow
You must remember this with total faith
That you are worth more than space

We all need your grace.

Impacts

Never know how deep or shallow
The crater will be upon meeting someone new
Sometimes you don't inspect the damage
Until after they change your world view
Upon inspection
You might find
A brilliant lake
Or a broken hole
That will force you to take
A different road you struggle to tread
But ultimately changes the world
BETTER from a place you dread

Counting

When you're mad, count to 10
When you're scared, count the fears you will conquer before you count the exits
When you are joyful, count the smiles as they spread
When you are powerful, count the influence you expound
When you're peaceful, count the flowers, the stars, the blades of grass.
When you're sad, it is said to count your friends, your family, and your blessings...

But when you're sad, you should also count:

All the times you were mad, but counted to 10 instead of hurting others
All the times you were scared but conquered instead of taking flight
All the times you were joyful and smiled instead of keeping to yourself
All the times you were powerful and shared instead of overpowering others
All the times you were peaceful and introspective instead of lackadaisical
All the times you were sad and COUNTED instead of letting go

But no matter how you feel, don't count yourself out!

My Heart Beats True

I stick to the beats as I move; following the notes of a song
I move steady as I go along
Sometimes I move fast like a racing train
Sometimes I move slow like the chorus refrain
But no matter the speed, I keep to the beat
Seemingly steady as if following a sheet
Yet there is no conductor, no first chair
Just faith that the beat is always there
A constant lub-dub from within myself
A beat everyone holds within themselves
But most only hear it in times of stress or fear
While I've spent my life following it, year after year

Dropping Pebbles

The pebbles, so smooth
Drop into the water with a plunk
The ripples are tiny as they expand
Yet, are not witnessed when they hit land
Waves break onto the shore with tsunami force
Clearing destruction to restore
All that wrong within its wake

The pebbles, so pretty
Drop onto the sand without a sound
They roll within the retreating waves
Providing a foothold for all that emerge from the sea
Yet you are not there to see
The turtles as they emerge or retreat
New life left at the beach

The pebbles, so small
Drop through the rocky shore with a clink, clink, clink
Falling between jagged rocks
Lodging themselves where they need to be
Yet you cannot reach into the rocks
To feel the starfish nourished within the pools
The dam protects them all

All you feel is the loss of pebbles
The grief overwhelms
Overtakes
Consumes

The pebbles are invisible when looking back
For they are underwater, covered in sand, or lodged between
    rocks
 The clean beaches, thriving turtles, and brimming tide pools do
    not remind you

The pretty, smooth, small pebbles lost

Yet, without you dropping pebbles…

Everything, Even the Kitchen Sink

Everyone notices the full kitchen sink
Some wash to clean
Some add to the pile
Some complain about the sticky plates, unclean glasses, missing
    silverware
Some turn their nose at the smell
Some just watch to see what happens

I threw everything in
Disregarding any mess
I just wanted it to be
NOTICED

This mess static in the heart
    Of their home
Infects everything
    Even the kitchen sink

Dialing In The Lens

Hitchcock was flawless
While I'm over here
Suffering from Vertigo
While looking through the Rear Window
Eying the pretty Birds
That have gone somewhat Psycho
Standing here
My perspective doesn't change
So I can't find
A movie worth watching

So I'm dialing in the lens
Changing the focus just so
Enough to bring the positivity forward
Blur the background
Into oblivion

The Oak

I see the oak
Strong, hearty just coming alive
After the cold, harsh winter

I watch the oak
Grow, spread, offering shade
Through the hot, stale summer

I hear the oak
Rustle, break, dropping acorns
Through the temperate, brisk autumn

I smell the oak
Smokey, fragrant, standing strong
Through the fire, burnt strike

I feel the oak
Bare, barren, preparing itself
To survive through the death of winter

The oak and I have something in common:
We both survive the cycle of seasons and storms

Growing Up

When I was a child, I wanted magic
To help me find my happy ending,
But part of growing up is learning
And expanding beyond what is trending

A movie about Arabian Nights taught me true
Wishes upon magic lamps sour
A book taught me finding 4-leaf clovers is hard to do
And of course those wishes don't flower

While I can still pretend there is hidden magic
I've grown up enough to know
That magic happy endings are only alive in books
Which I read to help me grow

The dangers of wishing too hard to escape
Will never let me enjoy the world where I am placed

Ledges

I stood on the ledge above open water
I looked down into the oblivion, and relief I craved
Then I heard a cry for help
I turned my head and saved

I stood on the ledge of a roof
I looked down to the STOP I desired on the street
Then I heard a friend gasp
I turned so I could greet

I stood on the ledge of a cliff
I looked down to the clouds swirling just below
Then I heard a crash
I turned to stop the flow

I wanted so bad to be at the end
But someone always stopped me
Every time I turned around
A person to help, saved me

What would the world be without my help?
I don't want to know anymore
Because this is after
I'm now beyond the before

But how did I get to the now?
I don't know the how...
I still have days I'm on the ledge
Wanting so desperately to go over the edge
Yet, there is always another heart beating
So close to mine, always needing
The help I seem to have as a gift
The little bit of light meant to lift
Spirits from the depths of dark
And leave them with a little spark

Now their lights are shining true
Their hearts are beating true
My love for them, always true

Wanda's Wet Toes

Rain pouring down
Puddles too deep
Wanda stepped in
Positivity always keep
It didn't matter
That Wanda had wet toes
She just smiled and said
"That's how life goes"

I strive for her positivity
While I'm stuck in the mud
But somehow I keep sliding
And stay mired in the crud

Wanda keeps telling me
The rain is here to cleanse
And life isn't all muddy
The sun will be back before it all ends

I look to the sky
Get rain in my eye

Wanda turns to me and says
"This rain is just today"
She hands me an umbrella
"Until the clouds go away"

So I stand, under protection
And wait for the rain to pass
While absorbing Wanda's strength
And knowing, this time, it'll last

Staying Still

There is a lack of wanting
    To do
    To be
    To thrive
    To learn
    To become
A melancholy if you will
Not deep, but on the surface and still
I'm staying; for the stillness to stop
From the pebble someone, somewhere will drop
Into the lake devoid of life
Stagnant and smelling somewhat ripe
I know staying isn't the way to be
But, I don't want... You see?
I crave a wave that will overtake
And leave me clean in its wake
But I stay here by a lake
Wondering if it is purposeful or by mistake
Please don't give me an answer
For this is still and still is all I feel

Days Always End

With a dawn shining true
My day starts anew
I bring yesterday along
Because it was such a deep blue
Today is somewhere I don't belong

I know the sun will set
I don't even have to bet
I will find my way to sleep
My mind wandering, I'll let
But the feelings I will keep

Then I rise with the dawn
A roaring, gaping, ugly yawn
I find myself facing a new day
A day I do my best to con
Keep you from asking "Are you ok?"

More times than not this plan works
Distractions are easy with my quirks
No one sees through to the pain
I know how to wear my smirks
My smoke's too thick to ascertain

As this day also ends, my feelings rolled tight
I find my way back to sleep this night
Aching because no one sees through
The mirror I use to block your sight
Tomorrow I wake with a deeper blue

Days always end
With or without a friend
I want to put these feelings down
But I seem stuck in this trend
Where my smiling face always hides a frown

I ask for your patience

When I asked, you gave
More than patience
YOU SAVED

Days always end
You can drop your feelings then
Now that I know how
I put them down

Days Always Begin

Days always begin
Not all of them will win
But If I start with a positive light
I have a better chance to feel alright

It isn't - It is

IT ISN'T

It isn't the words or even what they say
It isn't the grammar or the rules ignored
It isn't the format or the order within
It isn't the placement or white space on the page

What it isn't should be ignored and discarded

IT IS

It is the thoughts they evoke, the feelings they betray
It is the rhythm they set, the sound of a chord
It is the hope they ignite, the absolution of sin
It is the beating heart, the release from rage

For what it is awakens the soul, heals the broken-hearted

ALL OF IT

It is all of that and more
Write it for yourself and explore
Where the words guide you true
Soon you may see a clear picture of you

Echo Chamber

Does the past travel with me through time, filtered through you to
    come back at me again?
Like an echo chamber only built to reverberate the negative
Canceling out the positive while amplifying the remaining echoes
Like a DJ at a high school dance that can make the gym floor
    sound like the Sydney Opera House stage
Totally foreign but someplace I can't leave for the awe it inspires
Like a California death chamber eases me into a false peace right
    after the IV starts to drip

The difference between that chamber and this one is I hold a key

Once I recognize my chamber for what it truly is and understand
    what it is exactly doing, I can use my key to vacate
Instead of lying in wait for the final injection, I can leave and close
    the door behind me

Abandoning the echoes in the chamber so they can reverberate
    to themselves without an audience

Little Things

It is the random stranger's smile
The unexpected text after a long day
The kind word of a friend
The right word to say
The first breath of the morning
After a long night's sleep
The clouds gliding through the sky
It is poems about the promises to keep

These are the things that help me find hope
Even in the darkest room
After I decided
I survived my last kabloom
I keep finding hope, or it finds me
Even after I think it's gone
Just like the moonless night
Finds its breaking dawn

Playing With Words

You tell me you love my play, word by word
You tell me that you love all you heard
You tell me they help others grow
All the words I used to know
The ins & outs of my broken heart
Which I cannot separate from my art

I feel like a host, everyone gets something
    You get my words
    You get my recordings
    You get my books

Everyone gets a piece of my art
I'm still holding my broken heart
But the words are starting to stitch
My wounds are starting to itch
I know I'm healing from all that came before
And these poems, part of my lore

Because you said the words aren't me
Even if they tell my story
Because you said you could relate
Even if you don't share my fate
Because you said everyone needs to read
Even if I don't see their need

I'm grateful you took my words apart
To see how they play
I'm grateful you love my heart
No matter what the words say
I'm grateful you are cheering me on
Because I'm now moving beyond

I find that I am letting go
Of all that always hurt me so
Your view gave me a berth
For my pain and lack of worth

Same Coin

Sometimes I wish I could be indifferent
That way my heart won't beat with pain
But then I feel a beat full of love
So I stop the complaints

Two sides, one coin that indifference would steal
Stop my heart cold with lack of feel
Leave me blah and all that entails
Which seems harsher than when pain prevails

Indifference hangs black out curtains
Over windows to empathy while erasing burdens

Can't lose the loss without the love
Can't keep the love without the loss

Two sides, same coin

Wavering

I would be wasted, lying
On the verge of dying
But I am not

I wonder how many out there are like me
Wavering, alone as can be
But are not

I hope to find them now
Tell them I'm here, somehow
But know not

We all should live IN our life
No matter the strife
But can not

Let's get past the last not
Release the feelings caught
Because together we can

We are now unwavering

Fighting Blocks

I just learned you are the same way as me
Fighting for some sanity
I want to bond, but not over this
For it is wrong, this missing bliss

They beat into our heads how friends should be
And we just don't fit what they say, do we?
Friends through happiness not mental health blocks
Something exciting and cool like a band that rocks
But here we are instead
Strangers bound by common thread
Of mental health anguish
With a quest to distinguish
The darkness from the light
And for ourselves, we will fight

I'm glad I see it in the way I do
Otherwise we couldn't be friends so true
Let's just be friends like us
Let them all just eat our dust.

Positive Side

We tend to stick to the negative
And hold it tight
Even while it repels others
We cling with all our might
We neglect to look at the positive
While it is bigger than life
Attracting others
Saving us from our strife
Then someone comes along
Turns us around
Like lightning striking
We find our ground
That's what happened to me last night
While talking to friends about what makes the season bright.

Drops of Sorrow

I used to think rain drops meant the sky was crying
Dropping pain from the heavens above
I used to think dew drops were tears left by fairies
Who missed their chance at true love
I always thought of those tears
As drops of sorrow
Until my own pain
Filled up my today and tomorrow
Now I see the way the water washes
Cleanses the earth beneath the downpour
I see the way the water sustains
Feeds the plants; flowers more
I need the rain to remember
To display the rainbow bright
So I can get through my sorrow
And bask again in happy light

Stolen Confidence

Blending with the shadows
Stealing the brightest jewels
Weakening the sharpest tools
Silent as it roams the halls

The cat burglar then sells
To the highest bidder
So the jewels travel through
Private collections

Untraceable to all

Covered In Flyers

My psyche was a telephone pole, bare to the world
Until someone decided it would be a good place to advertise
Missing dogs
Murdered people
Help wanted ads with pull off strips for contact numbers
Pinning their tragedies over my successes
Hatred trying so hard to overwhelm my love
But my mercy hired a street team from the 90's
Mercy has a printing press
And a band worth promoting
Her street team is unrelenting
Ready with stickers to cover holes
Always diligently watching to ensure anything that distracts from
    the band
Is covered once again
The moment the person walks away
Thinking they successfully overtook something
The damage is reversed

Black

Black is a saturation, a hue
It has the power to change color
And a point of view

It is an armor I wear
Against all that you incite
Emotions too grand
You hope to ignite

So I'll wear black
Every day that I can
For it keeps me out of the fire
Away from the pan

Black is the chaos of color
Absorbing all that you spew
Too bad you don't see things
The same way I do

Holidaze

There are no words to explain
The way dates on the calendar feel
Watching them come and go
Dreading the ones that appeal
The days marked special
When printed on the press
Seem so cheerful to others
To me, they depress
I won't want to celebrate the year just past
Because it was harrowing, I didn't think I'd last
The hearts and flowers of St. Valentine
Break my heart a little more each time
St. Paddy's Day, full of song, parades, and cheer
Reminds me of that wasted time of beer
Easter and its gathering for rebirth
Sucks away all of my mirth
Memorial Day, celebrating the dead
Just reminds me of the life I dread
Flag Day is somehow always forgotten
Celebrating a flag, falling apart, rotten
Fourth of July with all of its explosions
Does its best to blow up my emotions
Then Labor Day comes around
Reminds me about working to the ground
Halloween with its frights and spooks
Is the only day, I wish it was a fluke
Because it is the day I can be someone else
Instead of me, where darkness dwells
Then the day when we give thanks
Gratefulness is hard when my emotion tanks
Hardest of all is what December brings
Everyone full of cheer, waiting for new year rings
I'd rather just curl up in a ball
Then face the calendar on the wall

Somehow, though, when last year was through
I felt something different, something new

I may not be ready for the holidays
But, I might see how they might find their ways
Into my emotions, shaded so blue
So I can experience them as I hope to

The Canyon

I always think that I'm not good enough for you
While thinking you are too good for me
The ravine these thoughts create
If real, could be seen from Outer Space
But unlike the Grand Canyon
This chasm
Is all in my head
I'm the only one aware of:
- The sheer walls of crumbling rock
- The changes in temperature from rim to floor
- The river's category six rapids flowing through the channel
- The beauty in the isolation
- The loneliness of the echoes from the vast ecosystem designed to repel

I carry it all with me
In packs, slogging along trails
Through the canyon
On treacherous paths far too narrow for more than one
I now have 50+ mules carrying the weight of all the baggage they entail
Snaking behind me
I don't feel their weight
Or see their struggle
But know they are there
For the rope I hold binds them too me

"When I get to the bottom", I tell myself, "I will let go."
But the trails are switchbacks
And down works in indiscernible increments
It will take longer than my lifetime
To reach the shores of cleansing waters

As I realize this, I turn around
I walk along my line of mules
Inspecting the packs
As I inspect, I find

The packs are easy to lift
Let them go slowly
One by one
On their own
As I watch the mules continue
Their journey
Weightless

I know then, I should have
Emptied the trash as it came in
Rather than pack onto mules
What is better left in bags
On the curb
For the trash man to pick up

Once the last of the packs
Hits the trail
The chasm closed
No longer repelling us

I mourn the time we lost
But make up for it in the love I give

I Know Now

How come you can't hear me
I'm screaming so loud

Because your screams are silent
Hidden in a cloud

How come you can't see me
I'm standing right here

Because you are so strong
There is nothing that you fear

How come you can't feel me
When I hold your hand

Because I need to let go
Don't you understand

Yes, I'm grown, but I still NEED
Your guidance, your love

I don't think so
You are so tough

But that isn't enough
I need you

I'm ashamed to admit, I know now
I need you, too

That was the conversation I wish I had
Before she was gone....
To tell her how strong and tough she was
To tell her how much I loved, because

I know now

She didn't know

Spiraling

Down the rabbit hole I fell
Spiraling toward the gates of hell
Deeper, deeper, darker, still
Let it take me, I have no will
No way to fight the onslaught
As I crash through the pain
No superhero will rescue
No one will explain
I'm stuck without an exit
I am beyond desperate

Throw me a lifeline
Keep me from decline
Be patient and giving
Keep me living

I hope I will survive

I see the rope you sent into my cave
It may or may not completely save
For I'm still scared of climbing out
And hold tightly to this crippling doubt

Thank you for climbing down here
And holding me through my fear
Exuding the patience I sought
It is more than I ever thought...

I know now, I can survive

Zesty

How do you go from holding the knife
To having an insatiable zest for life?
I ask myself this on the good days
Wondering how I mended my ways
I remind myself of this on the days gone bad
Convincing myself there's more to be had

The struggle is real and on the daily
Sometimes I win; sometimes I'm flailing
Still chugging along, mostly pretending
So you don't feel the coaster upending
Because you'll grab on and hold too tight
Like a famished pit bull in the middle of a fight
And just like the dog lost in the ring
I'm that close to what my thoughts will bring

But I smile instead and cling

To a sometimes faked zest for life
Wanting nothing more to do with that sharp little knife

Jumbled up

My are too thoughts many
I them write can't down
They me at come fast
I slow to them get can't down
They really aren't racing
They're jumbled all up
I a just on poured coffee my plate
Rather a in than cup

I center to tried myself
With yoga today
But I the second stilled
The to began jumbles replay
I'm be to struggling calm
To and chill relax
Breathe breathe in out
Jump tracks

That's to seem I how think
Until fall I asleep
Only wake to up
And jumbles the repeat

My getting is TBR* higher
The jigsaw's undone
The a is house mess
This not is fun

I asked for engines search help
And assistants virtual too
But the the list to added jumbles
I'm like stuck them to like glue

I took meds today
I think I'm ok

My thoughts were too many
I couldn't write them down
They came at me fast
I couldn't get them to slow down
They weren't really racing
They were all jumbled up
I poured my coffee on a plate
Rather than a cup

I tried to center myself
With yoga yesterday
But the second I stilled
The jumbles began to replay
I struggled to be calm
To chill and relax
Breathed in, breathed out
Jumped tracks

That's how I used to think
Until I took this med
Now I think in a line
Thoughts don't bounce in my head

My TBR* is smaller
The jigsaw's done
The house is so clean
Remembered to have fun

*To be read (books)

Connecting

I wish people were as easy to connect as dots

- Learn to count
- Find the next number
- Draw a line
- Make a pretty picture

Or even fours

- Review the grid
- Build a strategy
- Pick a slot
- Add a token
- Make a line

But they are not...

People are squiggly
Mushy in places
Hurtful in others
And completely unpredictable

There are no straight lines
Counting on them is hard

Connecting to them, even to four is harder
For bridges keep burning
Like I-85 after a homeless guy lit a fire under it
Melting away as if it was papier-mâché movie set
Not concrete, steel, and asphalt

I think part of me stopped trying
After reliving the destruction
Of lost connections
One too many times
Holding the inability to find the next dot
Against those who try to connect with me
Easier that way

Easier yes, lonelier too
Yet, the wall may be too high to dismantle now

But I want to feel a strong connection
More than anything
So I'm going back to dots
and fours
And counting on you to help me
Find connections
And make a pretty picture

Too Scary

I'm too scared to reveal
What is beneath my outer shell
Afraid to let you know
What is inside my inner hell

I'm worried you'll want to fix
The things I've just accepted
To keep myself sane
While hoping I'll be rejected

For this wall is here to keep you out
So you will never feel
The pain I've born through my torment
The thing that I cannot reveal

Not Able To

There are times I'm just not able to
No matter how desperately I want to
My ability limits me
Because it is an unability
Striking and somewhat flakey
Actually, completely unreliable
Shifting like sands of the dunes
Unlike stable Rosetta stone runes
Holding me captive in my bed
Twisting thoughts in my head
Curled up in a little ball
Clutching my blanket, staring at the wall
Wallowing in darkness with all the lights on

Praying the darkness will break with a dawn
Of the Artic Circle in summer when days don't end
So this darkness will shrink, bend
Into a rainbow
For I know it will with enough time
That's the reason for this rhyme
To remind me that this will pass again

That's my prayer, Amen

The Voice Inside

While I sit and say I don't know why
Or I don't know how
There has always been a voice deep inside
Telling me to keep going

When I'm about to fall apart at the seams
This voice always screams
So much louder than emotions
So much bigger than empty oceans
Swirling like water within a hurricane
Inducing a bitter migraine

To let it go unheeded is more painful
Than dealing with problems, dreadful

So I keep going on
Surviving
In the hopes that one day
I'll know the source of the voice
That keeps giving me advice

To keep going

Alone In a Crowd

I arrive before the crowd, say hello to everyone
Some of them brighten, some of them shun
I fixate on the ones who can't see past their nose
Instead of those who see my heart and the kindness it shows
I become more alone with every shunning person
With the growing crowd, I grow more certain
No one here likes me, even with their thanks
No matter what they say, my heart tanks
Why I think these thoughts so dark
Amid these friends who seek to spark
Love, community, and friendship for everyone
While I make myself exempt, the only one
That makes the rule
I'm purposefully alone in this crowd
That way they can't hurt me, it's not allowed

My Light

I stand on a stage
Bare, except for light
Sometimes I'm fully lit
Other times I'm in a single spot
There are times the lights follow me
Sometimes it is just the ghost that keeps me company

I stand on a stage
Bare, even to me
Sometimes it is dark
Other times darkness skirts the light
There are times the dark overpowers me
Sometimes it is just the ghost that keeps me company

I stand on a stage
Waiting for change
When I should be listening close
For the direction I'm told

"Get out there and make the most"

But I don't want to leave the ghost

So, I stand on a stage
Bare
Waiting....

Then someone comes along
They see my light
They sit, and enjoy the sight
And I know the ghost was right
This light was made for me
This is and always has been my light

My Darkness

My darkness clings to me like plastic wrap
Seals me in tight, but can let go in a snap
It clings to itself, but can also unravel
And it was made to travel
It reseals itself after several uses and comes on a roll
Wraps me up tightly, keeps me cold
It's clear so people can see me just fine
Even as I'm wound so incredibly tight
I can cut through it with a blade
So that the darkness becomes more of a shade
But there is always more from the box
Ready to replace it before I detox
From this plastic wrap that loves to cling
To my heart, my soul, my everything

Can you help me find the foil
So I can rid myself of the toil
Of fighting the cling that won't give way
No matter how far away I stray?

Self-Care

Everyone is droning on about self-care
Take an hour, take a day
Make yourself a priority
But I don't care about myself enough
It takes too much energy
For someone so unworthy

Do what makes me happy for an hour
What is that something?
There is no happiness
Nothingness
Even the things I used to love
Vanish and are replaced by …

How can I take care of myself
When all I want is a hole to crawl into?

But each time I get to the hole
I so desperately want
And start to crawl
I find a spark, a flower, a note, a person
That gives me a little of what I need
Just enough to change my wants

I'm still here
Unlearning my unworthiness
In small bits
As I learn to walk instead of crawl
And take care of myself after all

Celebrating

The quick brown fox jumped over the lazy dog.

Whew, I wrote something today.
It may be something someone wrote first, but it was still written.
Today.
By me.
It is a success, even if the smallest of one.
But a success none the less.
I'm celebrating it, because I need the reassurance
For the big wins won't arrive without
Little steps being taken

Without the writing, there'd be no poems.
Without the poems, there'd be no book.
Without the book.....

   I don't want to think about it.

I'm just happy I wrote SOMETHING today.
I'm celebrating.

Heart Configuration

I want so much that my heart not bleed
With this ache, this overarching need
To be loved, to be celebrated
To be more than underrated

To avoid the ache, I start doing more for me
Only to find the ache is growing

So I stop doing for me and wallow
Within the ache and the sorrow
Before I begin to see the light
That maybe I am not doing this right

I asked myself who will celebrate me and why
My need is too great to tell myself a lie
And I found that I don't celebrate people for being
I celebrate them for doing

So who would celebrate me for doing nothing
I am more than a sedimentary being
I want them to celebrate me for who I am
Someone kind, giving, patient, and BAM!

That's when it hit me, I have to give
All of myself, the life I live
So others can see, learn, and grow
Through me they will know

How to overcome their achy hearts
And find their own perfect parts

Walls

I was chipping away at the inside with an ice pick
Carefully examining each piece as it fell off the wall
Walking the dust off in the yard

You smashed through from the outside
With a wrecking ball

I wasn't ready

I'm now scrambling to clean up
Screaming about the mess YOU made
Rather than being grateful for your arrival
Hoping you'll back away without noticing

Franticly scrambling
Due to lack of chairs and cozy couches
Bay windows with cushioned seats
Next to the bookcase
With tea and scones

My screaming and scrambling becomes panic
While I ache for you to take the blame from me
For being unprepared

But you do neither

You accept my anger
Help me clean the mess
Hold me close and tell me it's OK
Furniture is overrated anyway
Until it is properly curated

We huddle on the cleaned floor
Sharing our newfound friendship
In the open air

Instead of holing up by myself in my walled off heart

Wishing

I wish my darkness was like the night
Routine
Fading in slowly
After a beautiful candy colored sunset
By which
Animals set their sleeping schedules
People set their working schedules
All of it associated with pleasure

But my darkness ebbs and flows like the ocean
Sometimes the waves only touch my toes
Others I'm completely underwater
Unable to find my way to the surface
Under the churning of the waves
And the thick foam
Its unpredictable tides
Tsunami waves
Floods
Hurricanes
Changing speed, direction
With rip currents pulling me further in
Whole beaches disappearing beneath my feet in hours
There is no routine
Except lack of one

Yes, I am wishing for night instead of darkness

But I'm also learning
How to swim
How to build a boat
How to sail
Ultimately so I can glide above the darkness
In a calm sea
Even if I am miles away from the shore

Guilt Trip

Today is the day I pack for my trip
With all the baggage I can hold
Every year, on this day
My trip has a story to behold

Instead of lounging on beaches
To best enjoy the summer sun
My trip keeps me wondering
What could I have done?
Would it matter if I listened more
Or if I took you to a distant shore?

Instead of climbing mountains
To see the view from the peak
My trip keeps me wondering
Why didn't you speak?
Would it matter if I urged you more
Or if we hiked to a volcano's core?

Instead of booking a week at a spa
To massage all my cares away
My trip keeps me wondering
How can it be that you didn't stay?
Would it matter if I hugged you more
Or if we found a new spa to explore?

The destination may never be the same
But it always has the same start
In remembrance of when you took yourself away
Leaving me here to stay

This day, the one I dread
Weighs so heavily on my heart
With all these questions of why or how
That no one can answer now

My trip is one I will take for the rest of my life
Because you are no longer alive

Coming and Going

"Close the door on your way out"
Doesn't apply to a revolving door
It just keeps spinning

Not unlike a hamster wheel
Except you are either
Coming in or going out
Or somehow stuck between

Coming in can be to shelter and safety
Or into a dark, empty building
Depending upon the day

Going out can wash you in sunshine
Or in pouring down rain
Depending upon the day

But you need to remember the door

Is still spinning

You can choose where you exit
Or you can stop the door in between
For a while
Really, as long as you need

Someone will soon
Unstick you from between
Either in or out
So you can again resume
Coming and going

Until you find someone
Who reminds you of yourself
When you were stuck
Because now you know how to help
Unstick them

Either in or out
Depending upon the day

Breakdown

We don't drive the same cars
Or the same way
Or even in the same direction
So, treating every car the same isn't possible
Even if the cars are EXACTLY the same

So, when the mechanic gets your car after a breakdown
They might not find the problem
For they drive differently than you
Usually in circles around the safety of the auto repair shop
Not necessarily through mountain passes
Iced over in winter with a 6% grade

Your drive requires different gears
Wearing down different parts

I could be driving the same make, model, year car
Built in the same factory
But, my car still has different parts than yours
Even if assembled the same way, on the same day

So, when one mechanic
Can't fix the breakdown
Feel free to find another mechanic
Do not feel unworthy
When they can't fix the car

They might not have the right toolbox
The car is worth more than you think

Gift Wrapped

We were labeled and put in a box
Wrapped up nicely, placed under a tree
Waiting for someone, anyone to open boxes
Either by brute force or delicately
While around us a party ensues
Celebrating all the attendees
How they gush when their dresses match their skin tone
How they admire lookalike guests near and far
They accept each other and promote successes
While we wait under our tree
For someone, anyone to pull us out of the box
Wrapped, labeled, for all to see

The party goers start unwrapping as the night grows dark
We are out of our boxes; we release our spark
We join the party, try to have fun
There are no labels, not a single one

We hand out labels, but take so much care
We make our labels pretty, define the rare
Everyone applauds as the last one is affixed
The party continues, everyone is transfixed

Once the labels appeared, their boxes weren't far behind
And the tree at the party is now so much prettier, well defined
Even though all the guests are now confined

Responding Rightly

I was just told to
Respond to the negative
With a positive
Math rules say this practice
Will increase the negative

But reality rules differ

There are, quite,
Opposite, in fact
The positive against the negative
Overcomes

With gratitude
Forgiveness
Love

Quiet On The Set

It is in the moment before the cameras roll
When everything's in place yet a little out of control
It is quiet and everyone sucks in a breath
Waiting for "Action", the quiet moment's death
Is it nerves or excitement of what's to become
A piece of moving art, a little something of everyone
That holds the air so charged and still?

This is the feeling I have facing things new
So much so I shake through and through
I seize up like a deer in headlights
Frozen into immobility avoiding delights
Standing at the threshold afraid to go in
Feeling deflated before I begin
Tramping these feelings with sheer force of will

I remind myself no one here wants to see me fail
And with that thought, I always prevail

Melancholy

Today, I slipped down the hill
Instead of rolling on the grass
At the bottom I just sat
Wanting friends to find me
I'm no longer bubbling with laughter
Or enjoying the sun on my face
I feel so foolish for slipping
Don't quite know how to pick myself up

My knees are scraped
My elbows are bruised
My ego is hurting
For I wasn't expecting to slip

The friends that were with me at the top
Vanished in thin air
Before they followed me down

But I'm just taking a break
I'm not good at sitting
Alone

Since my friends left me
After laughing and shaking their heads
Without even looking down the hill

After my break, I become more than I was
And I begin to love myself, just because

Overthinking It

I can do it
Wait, no I can't
I'm stopping
Before I start…
To consider
All the ways
It goes right
It goes wrong

Wait, I'm behind
I need to catch up
I don't have a plan
For this
Left field is too far left
To be right
Can we go back?

Let me start again
I can't do it

Yes I can
If I just go
Without thinking

New Brand of Agoraphobia

I want to be out in the world not stuck in my phone
I want to experience things outside my comfort zone
But every time I step outside the phone goes with me
No matter the place or time or event, it's insisting
With flattery, complaint, bothersome non-sense
Or pesky authenticators that cause problems
Every day, the blasted phone intrudes
AI now controls my interludes
There is no getting lost to find peace
There is just this overly smart technology
Turning me inside out
Filling my head with doubt
Keeping me tied up in knots
Looking for imaginary sub-plots
I'm too scared to go explore
So, here I stay, behind my door

Tornadoes

My emotions are a whirlwind
Tornadoes whipped from slight breezes
Wreaking destruction
My whole life freezes

Nothing is done
My house is a mess
My job's on the line
My pay is now less

I can't grab hold
For the winds are too fast
I'd thought they'd die down
But they seem to last

Where are the trees
To cut the wind
Slow it down
So control can begin

Where do I get them
I do not know
Can you help me?
Or do I need to make them grow?

The whipping wind
Still won't abate
It's tearing everything apart
There went the gate

The wind took the house
Lock, stock, and barrel
Now I'll live like cats
All sorts of feral

Accepting the Divergence

Darkness overtakes a little bit at a time
Like these little harmless pieces of foam
Shredding from a rocket
Along the body of a shuttle

The pieces of foam are light
They break apart in your hand
With such little effort
They don't do any damage

At first...

These harmless intrusions into safety
Become acceptable
Because they aren't dangerous
They are light and small
They break apart so easily
And they bounce

But as these acceptable pieces of foam
Keep flying
Keep bouncing
They start to dent the safety
Of reinforced barriers, once so strong

If care isn't taken
The foam can punch a hole big enough
So the shuttle can't get back to Earth
Without bursting into flame

Is accepting the divergence into darkness
Allowable?
Maybe, to a point
But if you are so accepting
How will you know
The point where the foam,

So light
It breaks apart in your hand
With such little effort and doesn't do any damage
Becomes a deadly weapon?

Tread carefully within the darkness
It is easy to get lost here
Stuck, circling the Earth
In a shuttle too damaged by foam to arrive
Without bursting into flame

- In remembrance of Space Shuttle Columbia, February 1, 2003

Complaintantcy

Complaining too much
Tends to drive a deaf ear
Especially when the complaints
Are not what I want to hear

The complaints become a routine
Just part of my day
Until they become silent
Because they are taken away

The silence is a relief
For it means no more complaints
But I did nothing to resolve them
I just used great restraint

To keep from fighting back
Or fixing the issue
From shedding any tears
Or having a breakthrough

But the silence doesn't signify
An acceptance of terms
It means there is now an empty vault
No longer giving out returns

So while I heard complaints
I left them in complacency
Keeping myself unchanged
And my heart in vacancy

Not Safe

A psychologist once told me
I'd be safer walking the streets of Hollywood than living at home
With my family
It wasn't safe

Yes, I lived in my car
That was safer
It wasn't safe

A doctor once told me
I'd be safer living in a battered women's shelter than living
With my man
It wasn't safe

Yes, I lived on the run
That was safer
It wasn't safe

Now I have my own home

The news keeps telling me
The world is not safe...

I have nowhere left to go.

But, I found safety.
It isn't hiding or moving, or running
It is with love and people who are loving
Safety abounds in numbers
When people are true to one another
Standing, working, striving with and for each other

That is safety.

I am safe now

Emerging from a Darkened Theater

Exiting a matinée is always disorienting
You expect it to be dark, late at night
Yet, the sun is out shining brightly
Your brain thinks, "This can't be right"

Your eyes scream from the pain
Caused by the searing sunshine
Your first instinct is to go back in
To the known place where you were fine

But your ticket is no longer valid
It has already been used
You are locked out on the sidewalk
Somewhat confused

So you try to remember where you parked the car
Even though your brain is looking for the moon
You wander up and down all the aisles
Hoping you will find it soon

When you finally spot the car
You race to the doors
Only the car looks so different
Then you realize it isn't yours

Three rows over, you find it again
This time, checking the plates
Seems all is well this time around
And you're in the right place

Yet now, you don't remember where the keys are
Your pockets are empty
Turns out they are on your thumb, against the cup
Bought with your last twenty

Sitting behind the wheel, you don't know where to go
Because you can't go back from whence you came
The world is so different now
You will never be the same

So you sit and wait in the lot
Until the day catches up to your thoughts
The stars start shining, the moon is now up
And your brain resumes after the pause

Being Introspective

I'm quiet with an annoyed facial expression
Struggling over how to convey
And how to express my thoughts
Spiraling through my head like an endless news channel banner
Flashing 24/7
When the camera turns
The perception is warped
Because the lighting wasn't set
And the make-up artist didn't blend
The director rolled before the prompt
So the audience switches off
Walks away
Even while the camera is still rolling
And the banner is still flashing

Layers of Paint

It starts blank
Before the artist adds color
With every layer, depth is added

All of this is crap that needs to be destroyed

For it is ART

The layers only make the depth so deep...

What color is this?

My Darkest Time

That time weaves a web inside my brain
So every thought repeats its refrain
Paints every action and reaction
So every movement displays its refraction

The light does not diminish its power
Because its fossilized within its hour
Forever holding court amid my emotions
Even without any of my devotions

To keep the darkness from leaking in
I need to understand where to begin
Learn what thoughts the darkest time changes
Keep my actions and reactions within proper ranges

Seems easy on paper, written in black ink
Not so easy when the spider still weaves in all I think
So I work daily towards my grandest goal
Drop the darkest time in the deepest hole

I Stayed

Even after everyone else gave up
Because I said I would
Because you asked me to
Because I wanted to
Because the weather's nice
Because the weather's bad
Because someone needed to help clean
Because I fear what will happen to you if I left
Because...

All the reasons there ever is or was

I just wish you wanted me to stay

Ball of Yarn

Unraveling like a ball of yarn
In a cat's paw
Thrown in no discernible direction
Unrolled a little at a time
Through every room
String around all the fixtures
Chewed through in places
Separated into strands in others
Knocking over the small stuff
Getting tangled under the big stuff
Completely given free reign
The cat with the yarn
Makes life impassible
But not impossible

All I need is the right distraction
For the cat
And the right slicing instrument
For the yarn

To get myself close to where I was
Before I gave the cat the yarn

Foggy Mind

The fog rolls over his mind
Like the hills of San Francisco
Rolling in, slowly
Hiding a bit of shore at a time
Falling back upon itself
Near the tallest peak

When the sun starts to shine
The fog burns off

Most days are sunny
In the summer

But lately, the cloud layer is thick
Between the sun and the fog
No match for the sun's heat
The fog grows thicker still
And unlike my skin
It doesn't burn anymore

The light in the lighthouse
That used to guide the way
Is spinning slower now
Soon, the boats will crash into the shore
Hidden within the fog

No one will notice the boat's approach
Until it is too late....

So enjoy the sunshine today
Tomorrow's going to be bad

Another (Part 1)

AS IF I NEED ANOTHER

Drink
To obliterate my feelings
To black out the world

Person
To pull me apart, piece by piece
To stomp on my heart

Reason
To end things
To be done with the hassle of it all

Another (Part 2)

YES, I NEED ANOTHER

Drink
Of Water
To nourish my body

Person
To help
To feel useful

Reason
To begin again
To live

Never About Me

The song is never about me
But always for me instead
To learn the ways of broken hearts
And get out my head

The song is never about me
But describes what I've felt
It is uncanny with its power
How it just makes me melt

The song is never about me
But somehow the song has always known
Who I am; who I've loved
And how much I've grown

The song is never about me
Which sometimes makes me mad
Because I want what's in the lyrics
All that I've never had

The song is never about me
But changes my mind all the same
With enchanting beats and bridges
That allow me to forget my name

The song is never about me
But always for me instead
I have to remember that
And stay out of my head

Testing 1,2,3

I'm still stumbling around in the dark
Trying to find the way to spark
Striking out left and right
Beginning to feel I'll never see the light
Still, trying one more time

Hoping to entice friends
Connections greater than an ends
But somehow always fall short
Because I try tools to contort
And end up seeming a pantomime

Like someone fake who fails to show
Who I am and what I know
To a level you can believe
Because it is difficult to conceive
What I know and what I've seen

Hiding myself was never my goal
I want you to see the depths of my soul
To witness the strength I wield
Against life on its battlefield
And know EXACTLY what I mean

Testing, testing 1,2,3
Can you hear me?
Testing, testing 1,2,3
Is this thing on?

Counting Blessings

Blessings are relative
To the person counting
A person without a home may count the roof
And the walls
While the housed may only count the home
A penniless person may count every penny
And the nickels, dimes, and quarters
While the rich may only count the dollar
A faithless person may count every single thing
While the faithful may only count every person

We have to remember
We are truly blessed
Even if we fail to count

For we are all alive

Anywhere, Anytime

The words flow
As easily as the tears
Full of love
Beyond any fears
But they stay static on the page
Never getting past the stage
Of being

Yet the words still flow
As easily as water into the sea
Full of fear
Beyond all of me
But they stay still within the lead
Just barely getting out of my head
Of being

And the words continue to flow
As easily as blood from the vein
Full of anger
Beyond any aim
But they stay trapped within the ink
Just barely sharing what I think
Of being

They appear anytime, anywhere
Even on the bathroom floor
I must sit and write them out
I cannot ignore
Before they disappear
Even if they stay trapped
They may be the wood that turns to stone
Here long after my last
May bring solace to someone I'll never meet
Or get woven into a song
Of being

The Universe Beyond

Twists & Turns
You matter

I remember that movie about being a parent
Where the grandma spoke about a roller-coaster
With its up and downs, twists and turns
I compared it to life
Singing its praises

I remember that movie about being single
Where that guy at the end made sure
His girl felt she mattered
I compared it to life
Telling all, you matter

I remember a movie about an alien
Where the girl at the end killed everything in sight
I compared it to life
Realizing I don't want us to take ourselves
Into the universe beyond
With greed, or ill will towards others

Just love and connection

Starry, Starry Night

Floating in the pool
Viewing the stars
I couldn't help but think
Of all that bars
Us from connecting to the universe
So grand and vast
Our cities and towns so full of people
Yet our lights cast
The opposite of shadows
A barrier of light
To keep us from seeing
The starry, starry night
I need to connect again
To the great beyond
This is what I think
As I float in a pool that should be a pond

Fix It In Post

Throw the crap to the walls
See what sticks
Do not care if it makes sense
You might be surprised at the results

You can always fix it in post

Karaoke Night

Sitting at the table
Listening to others karaoke
Sung, not so well
By people I do not know
Singing along from my chair
Feeling I sing worse than them

Yet I still sing and so do they
Belting every note from our hearts
Making us feel every song
Because the music
Is melting our walls

I'm not sure what the magic is
But it is something
That only happens
On Karaoke Night

I Can't Quit

I try
I fail
I give up, only to be awarded…

> I try to write like those heroes of yore
> Shakespeare, Chaucer, Frost
> But before
> I start I have to stop
> The meter is all wrong.
> I think of topics to grace these lines
> Love, Death, Despair
> Yet, besides
> I think too much to drop
> The words are all wrong.
> The more I try, the worse I feel
> This writing thing will never be real.
> Taking patterns from what I've read,
> Letting them wander through my head,
> Keeping the whole poem on the page,
> I give up, even at this stage.
> I don't know how they did it and never will
> Because I give up climbing this hill
> I will never live up to the greats.

I run away, only to be scolded…
> Like a five-year-old with a suitcase
> A savior gives chase
> Leads me back, holding my hand
> I keep crying "You don't understand
> This it TOO hard, I have to quit"
> "You don't get to, that's just it
> There is someone, may not be today
> That NEEDS your words and what they convey
> Think of Dickinson, whose work was hidden away
> Look what happened when those words saw the light of day…
> That could be you, if you just stay"

These echoes ring through my head every time I say
"I QUIT"
So I don't... I can't even try anymore.

Heart Beats

I used to pluck words out of thin air
Not worrying about how you'd care
Only worrying about the beats
That led to the heart

I used to string words together in rhyme
If for no other reason than time
Only reasoning with the beats
That led to the heart

Used to is so long ago now
Words are disconnected somehow
Locked in cabinets behind glass
Because someone, somewhere was so brass
To steal the words and their meaning
Without ever gleaning

True intent

These stolen words, housed under lock and key
Have more than one intention, see
For they cause a moment to ...

STOP

And reflect
Upon where we were, how far we've come
To remember all that's said and done

Keeping them hidden, locked away
Will stop the beats, oh so true
Will stop new mind from the sway
Of what was then, or all we do
To prevent the then from becoming new

Since the words cannot be plucked
Without someone to review
My ink stopped flowing
And the beats stopped growing

The drum, now silent
There's no marching
Only following

Without heart beats

Looking At Death

The view you see of death
Depends upon the side you are on
When experiencing it you don't want to share
When losing someone you don't want their life done

Death is a word that strikes fear
As we cling so tightly to our world
But as we live our lives so brilliant
Towards it we are always hurled

Those who grieve a death of a loved one
Don't know what to do
Should they surround themselves with others
Or hide themselves from view

Those who have died…

Don't Test Me

All I WANT to do is hit someone HARD
All I want to do is hurt someone for something they didn't do
It isn't fair
But it is what I FEEL
Exacting anger
Which needs to be directed at someone
And that someone cannot be me
So it might as well be you

This is what I fight
Each time my anger surges
I must find a way to stop
Quell these abusive urges

I read books
Talk to experts for advice
Retrain my brain
Learn how to think twice

But I'm still trying
To remember my resolve
So don't test me
For my anger may not dissolve

Platforms

Before joining the platforms
I anticipated events
I was always with people
I had a few good friends

But each event is now
Fraught with anxiety
Because there is a layer
Between you and me

It twists and turns
Shows only slices of life
Sarcasm and irony
Birth so much strife

The friends I now have
Are blips on a computer screen
They comment and like
Share but are never seen

They care, and then they don't
They jump with the trends
I can't keep up
With my hundreds of friends

I fear going out
To be seen in the wild
Someone with a camera
Could just recompile

Moments not meant
To be seen in that way
Twisting of words
No context of what I say

I want to destroy
The platform and forget
But the want will ensure
We never had met

Paintings

When you donate belongings to charity
Those belongings are gone forever
Onto a new home, bringing joy to others

Trauma is like a donated painting
One that leaves a clean spot on the wall
With a nail still piercing the wallpaper

Survival means the paining is gone
But the mark it made remains

You can't clean the wall around the spot
For the years have etched the difference
And the hole will forever remain
Even after it was filled

You can only change your reaction to the spot
So
Hang another painting
Of beauty, love, and kindness
A painting to overshadow the trauma
Even if it uses the same nail

Emotional Soup

Everything was thrown in
At once
Heated at high
Left to boil over

The liquid evaporated too quickly
Solids burned to a crisp
Fused to the pot

No manner of scrubbing
Can remove the burnt taste
Everything cooked in the pot since
Has remnants of the boil over

If only there was patience
To let it simmer
For the slow melding
Into perfection

If only... cannot change the pot

But the pot cannot be thrown away
It must be either taken as it is
Or scraped out again
Sanded down to raw metal
And re-seasoned

The process takes a lot of work
Is it worth the time
Or is it better to eat burnt soup forever?

Inner Thoughts, Revised

Racing through your mind
Confusing, controlling
Intertwined

Erratic and fleeting
Sometimes true
Hormones change them
But they are not you

Separate the good from the bad
Hardest struggle
Within
For with every thought
The fight begins

With every day
A chance to redeem
All you are
And every dream

Think great thoughts
Hold them strong
Discard the bad
As they happen along

Keep what you need to succeed
Better your world from inside out
Erase every
Single
Doubt

Carpet Pull

Standing in a room of wall to wall carpet
Feeling I'm on solid ground

Until the tacks gave out
Then I found

The carpet gone, sand beneath my feet
And the overwhelming feeling of utter defeat

I didn't move a muscle, the carpet was just gone
If it was a rug, I'd understand, but this is so wrong

The tacks are not broken and not one is bent
So how did they let go? Who knows where the carpet went?

I try to stand, but here I sit
Screaming, "Do I deserve it?"

The echoes don't answer
So I have to find myself
A new carpet to stand on
That isn't in this hell

Trying To Be Me

Trying to be me
In a sea
Of glitter and pinks
Standing out in my black
Staying myself, won't go back
Always unapologetically
Without shame or remorse
No matter the outward recourse
Seemingly angry until I smile
Wanting more with every mile
I'm overweight by the scale
But happy within always regale
Of times like these
Being me
Succeeding

Until the looks up and down
Cause me to rethink myself
Do they see my weight bulging out of my clothes
Do they see the evil thoughts flying through my head
Are they judging me by their thoughts
Or am I judging me by mine?

Life Is A Dance

Step, step, step, twirl
Step, step, twirl, trip
Glide, together
Glide, apart

Count it out
1, 2, 3, 4
5, 6, 7, 8

Slow down, speed up
Slide to the right
Slide to the left
Fall

Wait, let's try another
Grab your partner, do-si-do
Swing around, don't you know?

Forward, back, hands on hips
Watch your frame
Dip
Land flat on your back

Even when life is a dance
It must be learned
You won't know every twist
You won't know every turn
Give yourself time
To trip and fall flat
Get yourself up
Return to the dance

Because life without movement
Stagnates like water
Learning to keep moving
Will always be harder

Tapestry

Finding the common thread
Is not as easy as it seems
Because the patterns are infinite
And there are seams
While the thread is sewn through
The directions vary
So the way is lost
When the emotions won't carry
But I keep pulling
At every thread
To help, heal, and love
You, my friend.

Realities

Looking at your reality
Wishing it was mine
Instead of working toward
A goal defined
Commiserating
I cannot reach
The reality that I want
Completely lacking in action
While putting my letters in pretty font
I point the blame to other things
For my inaction isn't at fault

And the chain of blame expands
Beyond the scope of one
To every reality
That looks even remotely fun
Because they have what I want
Without putting in the work
And everyone with these realities
Calls me a jerk

I just don't understand
Why is this all on me?
All I want is what you have,
And I want it work-free.

Marginally Accepted

I am not marginalizing your life
I analyze it, comparing it with my own
Return the results to you
In math terms
Not emotionally charged terms
For comparison can be proven
Greater than <
Less than >
= to
Nothing

Adding in the emotions
Is not something I do
For anxiety, depression, fear, anger
Cause the vectors to bend
Break the algorithm

I like my lines straight
Even as I like my black and whites gray
That is my confusion
Sorry I'm set in my way

I don't mean it to be hurtful
Or make you feel less
By disregarding emotional response

I hurt less

Stale and Stagnant

The bread was left out
Opened on the counter
The kitchen was dry
So the bread became stale

The water was left un-drunk
Uncapped on the end table
The TV room was humid
So the water became stagnant

Unattended and unmoving
Stale and Stagnant

Can be overcome
By action

Create croûtons with the stale bread
Refresh gardens with the stagnant water

If not for yourself
Then, for others

For we can all use a little crunch
In our fresh salads

Reaching Out

Every time I reach out for help
My hand gets slapped away
Every time I reach out for sanity
My hand gets burned

Each time I ask to be useful
I am turned away
Each time I ask for forgiveness
I am unforgiven

There are only so many times
I will put my hand in the box
Trusting that the box won't hurt

I'm at that point now

I'm coiling within
Like an animal in pain
Hiding and licking my wounds

Is is any wonder that I lash out to my rescuers?

Learned behavior is always repeated
Until it is unlearned

Simply Strike Love

Someone once told me
"Simply strike one love"
As if it was a simple task to dismantle
The apartment
The stairwell
The bedroom
The kid's room
The hospital room

Unscrew it from the floor
Roll it backstage
Remove every bolt
Every wire
Every lamp
Every piece of bric brac or knick knacks
Collected within
Categorize it
Store it in the depths of darkness
To be reassembled for another lifetime
For another love

As if doing so didn't crack open my heart
For there were lives in
The apartment
The stairwell
The bedroom
The kid's room
The hospital room
Lived for a thousand reasons
To touch a thousand hearts
Like mine, but not

Simply striking love
Cannot be done
For it lives forever

Tomorrow....

I am either comparing my yesterday to today
Or comparing my today to my yesterday
I am not thinking about tomorrow

I am either commiserating what is now
Or reminiscing over what was then
I am not hopeful about what is next

Always looking back
To review what next step I take
To feel what feelings there are
To know who matters

Looking forward is hard
For there are disappointments there
Failures
Loneliness
Especially if I do it wrong
I will be cast through the gates of hell

I'd rather stay where I am, in the knowing
Of what was yesterday and what is today

For tomorrow isn't even guaranteed

Dark Tunnel

The light at the end of the tunnel is just that, light
The shape of the tunnel is unfamiliar
And the light shifts
As the clouds pass between the Earth and sun
Or the Earth rotates on its axis
Or the moon phases out

You distrust your eyes
Your knowledge suspended
As your screams echo back
Without answer

You begin bouncing off the walls
Looking for the RIGHT way out
Finally believing deeper is the way to go
Digging so deep the light is no longer visible
The darkness now swallows you whole
Your questions start echoing back as answers
Garbled due to all the new angles

Even from within the hole
You are the answer
You cannot see

The canary no longer sings
Because his song went unheeded

Averting Attempts

I spent my 9th month in the womb
Averting an abortion attempt

My childhood, I spent averting abuse
My teens, averting familial relationships
My twenties, averting domestic violence
My thirties... averting memories of all that came before

My forties, I began averting self-inflicted wounds

All the averted attempts
Like rejection letters
Collected on a spike
Every pierced attempt
Kept me here

FOR YOU

There is no other way to explain
The vast amounts of pain
Through all the different phases
Documented in these pierced pages
Have come to be
Other than a broken heart's relief...

But I cannot believe this is all for me
Which is why I am sharing with you
All the attempts I've lived through
So you can survive your attempts too

A Seat For You

My safe place is a black box
Lights hang from the ceiling
99 seats sit empty within
I stand in the center
Bask in the red glow of the exit signs

They say to avoid blackness
In safe places in your mind
For it will only make life seem darker
But I don't see black as darkness
Never have

I see turquoise, teals, and greens
I'm reminded of Caribbean Seas
As I look at the absorbent shade
I see chaos, a lack of patterns
A puzzle to figure out

I know I'm not done yet when I retreat here
For here, I can create anything within my black box
On my blank slate
And tell any story
And someday, 99 people will take a seat to enjoy.

Look, I've saved a seat for you.

Stay

Please stay
I ask this even as I struggle to stay
I want to run away
Hide from the sharp edges of life
That keep cutting
Maybe not as deep
But just as painful
Or in some cases, more so

Please stay
I ask this because I need a reason
I want to go away
Remove myself from the rocky terrain
That keeps scraping
Maybe not through my calluses
But still painful
Or, in some cases, more so

Please stay
I ask this

Please stay
I ask myself

I stay for you
You stay for me
Deal?

The End

It only takes one
Just one
That's what I tell myself
One.
Next thing I know
One hundred…

I hope to reach
ONE
With my 100
Did I reach you?
Are you still here?
Should I reach for another
One?

Suicide Hotline

If you or someone you know is struggling or in crisis, help is available. Call or text **988** or chat 988lifeline.org. Caring counselors listen and provide free and confidential support 24/7.

Donate to 988 prevention efforts here: https://988lifeline.org/donate/

Acknowledgments

First and foremost, I need to thank Karen Fuller, M.S., LMFT, RPT for not only encouraging me to write these poems but reviewing them for inclusion in this book. When I started writing the poems in this collection, I scared myself silly thinking I was on the verge of total darkness. Karen pointed out the light in every single poem. She kept telling me to keep writing, especially as the light got brighter. With her help, I am stronger. I now know the darkness will pass ~~when~~ if it comes back my way again.

Secondly, I need to thank Yong Takahashi and Bridget Purdy for reading through the first, unedited draft. Your insights, support, changes, and ENCOURAGEMENT have made this a collection I am proud to share with the world.

Next, a big cheer for Phyllis Benton! Your cheering is in the back of my mind every day. Without it, I wouldn't be brave enough to actively cheer this book on and tell people they need to read it. Your faith in my work, and in my heart, is now in my soul. Thank you!!

An extra special thank you to my family: My husband, for continuing support and putting up with my moods. My daughters, for pushing me to keep writing and showing me I am a better person than I think I am. For all of you putting up with microwave meals, getting to restaurants just before they stopped serving, and keeping positive. It'll be better from here on out.

A BIG SHOUT OUT to Dee, Kim, Andre, and Robin. Your efforts in prevention healed my heart and pushed me towards documenting it so I can help others like you help me. You don't even know how much your presence in this world means to me. Seeing your wonderful posts online makes my day every day. Keep sharing the love!

And lastly, you dear reader, thank you for staying with me on this journey. I wouldn't have it any other way.

DON'T GO ; STAY